The Heart of the King
Coloring Book

Daniel King

Unless otherwise indicated, all Scripture quotations are taken from the *New International Version*. Copyright 1973, 1978, 1984 by the International Bible Society. Used by permission of Zondervan Bible Publishers.

The Heart of the King
By: Daniel King
Illustrated by: Emiliano Villani

ISBN: 1-931810-21-4

© Copyright 2015, Daniel King
All Rights Reserved.

No part of this book may be reproduced, stored in a retrieval system, or transmitted by any means, electronic, mechanical, photocopying, recording, or otherwise, without written permission from the author.

King Ministries
PO Box 701113
Tulsa, OK 74170
1-877-431-4276
www.kingministries.com
Daniel@kingministries.com

Once upon a time there was a King.

The King was known throughout his land as a wise, kind, and generous ruler. He had a wonderful heart full of love and compassion for all his people.

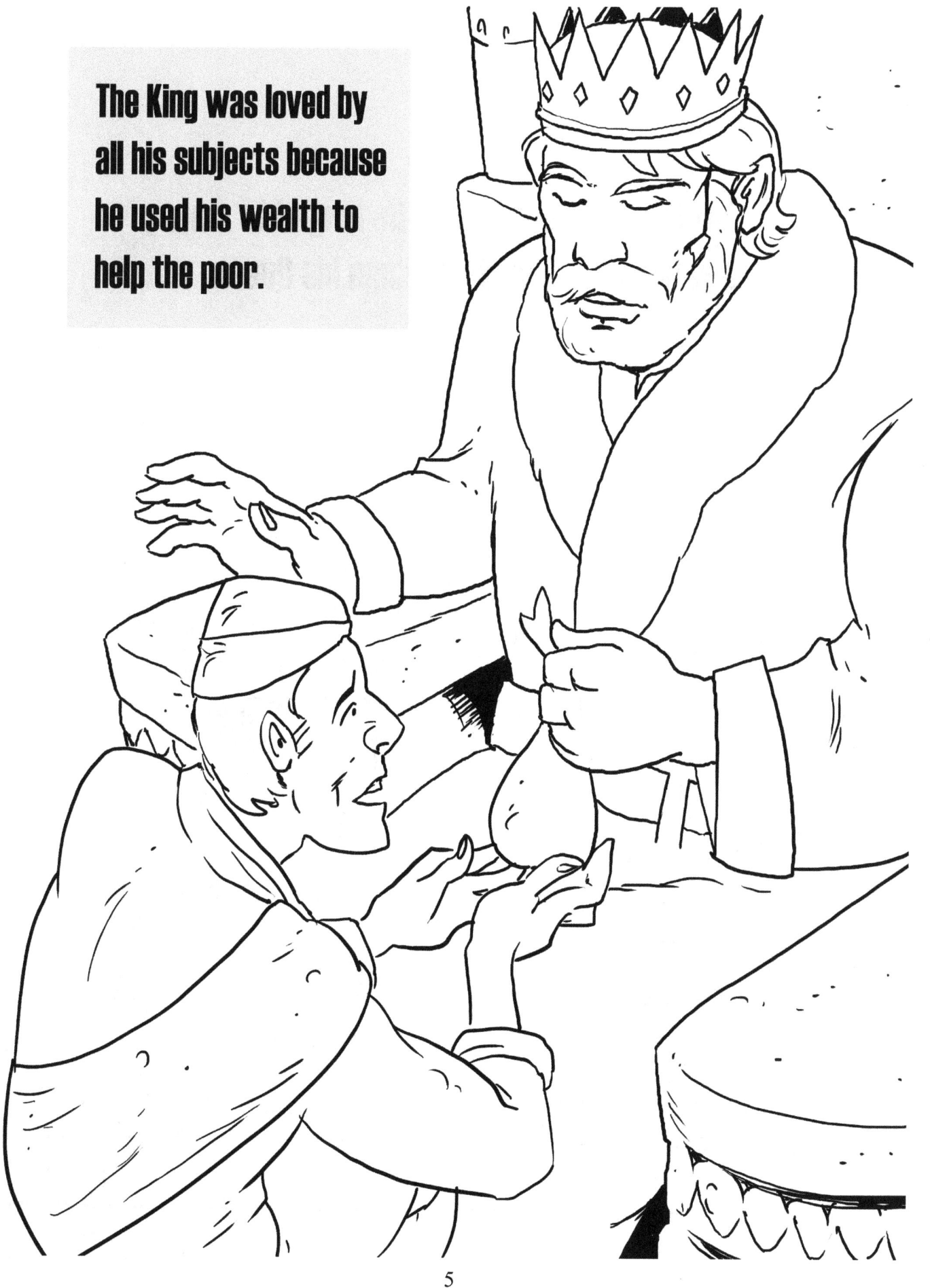

The King was loved by all his subjects because he used his wealth to help the poor.

But the King was lonely. He longed to marry a woman who would become his Queen.

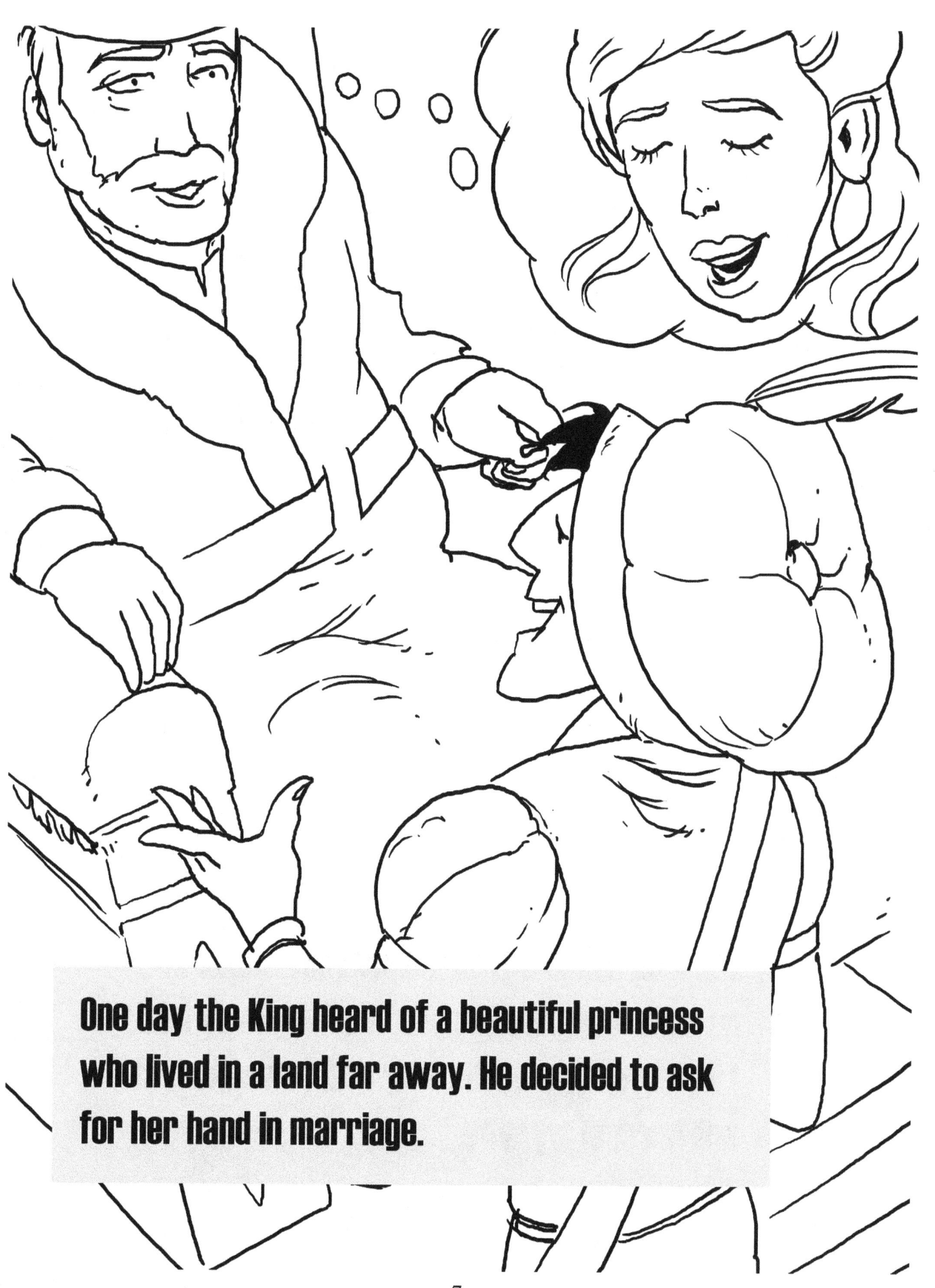

One day the King heard of a beautiful princess who lived in a land far away. He decided to ask for her hand in marriage.

The King called a trusted servant. "Good sir," he said, "I am sending you to a far away land. I want you to ask the beautiful Princess if she will become my wife."

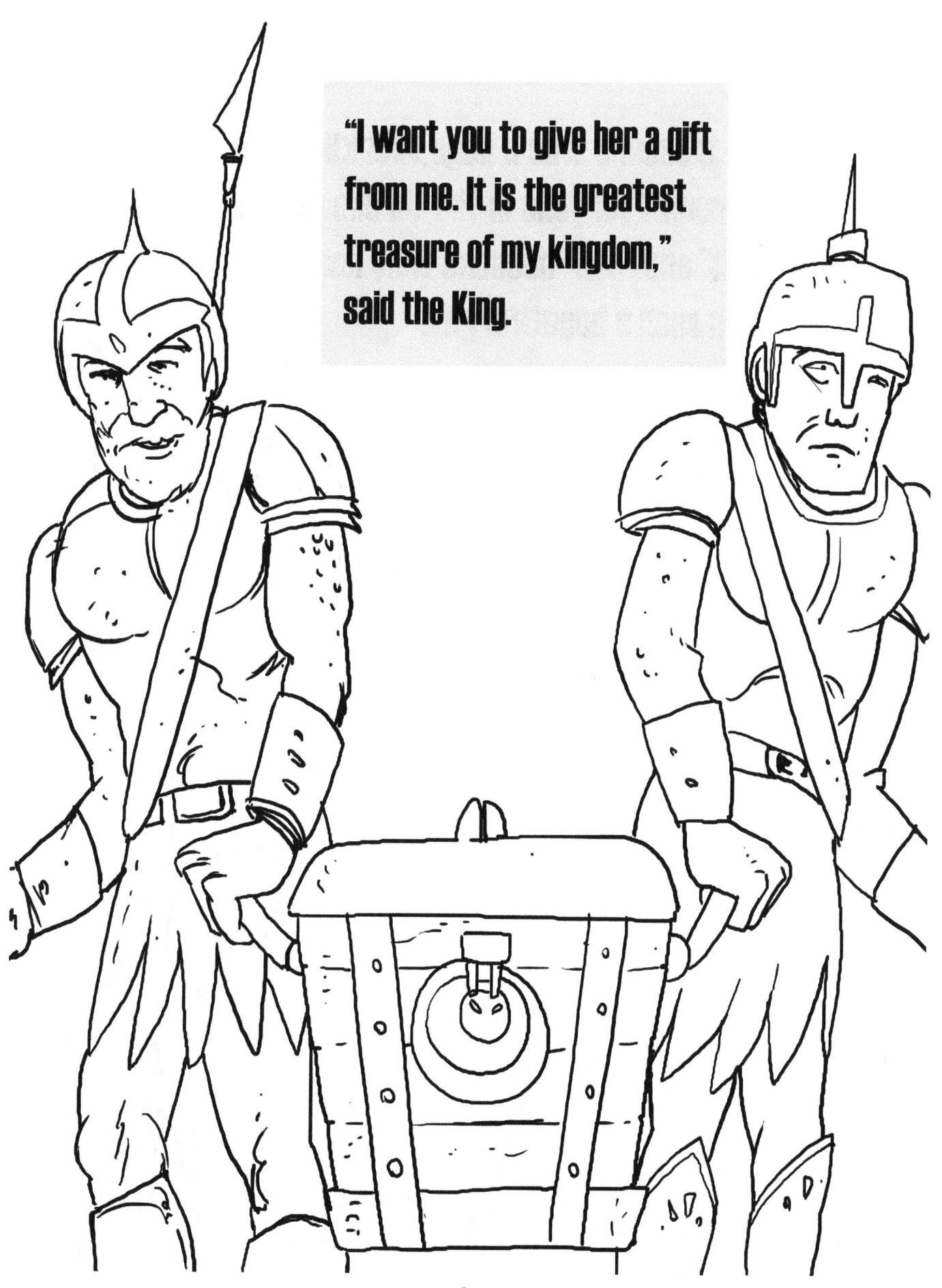

The treasure was a huge sparkling diamond. Everyone in the throne room said, "Ooh" and "aah" because they had never seen such a beautiful gift.

As the servant left the city, the people cheered for him because of the magnificent gift he carried. Twelve other servants accompanied him on the journey.

They crossed deserts, mountains, rivers and valleys. From time to time, the servant peeked at the valuable diamond he carried.

The servant became proud as he thought about his assignment. He thought, "I must be mighty important to be chosen to carry such a wonderful gift."

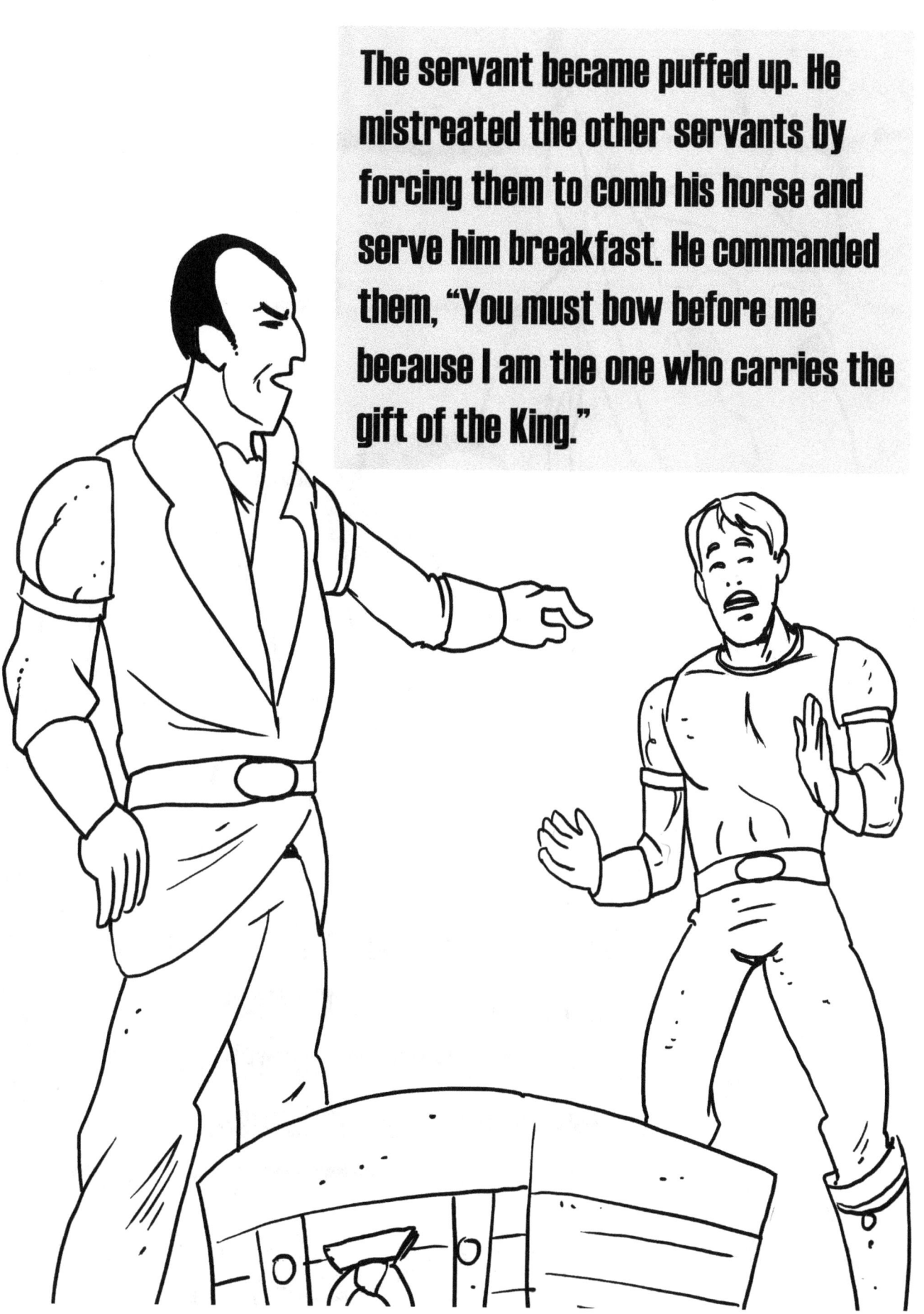

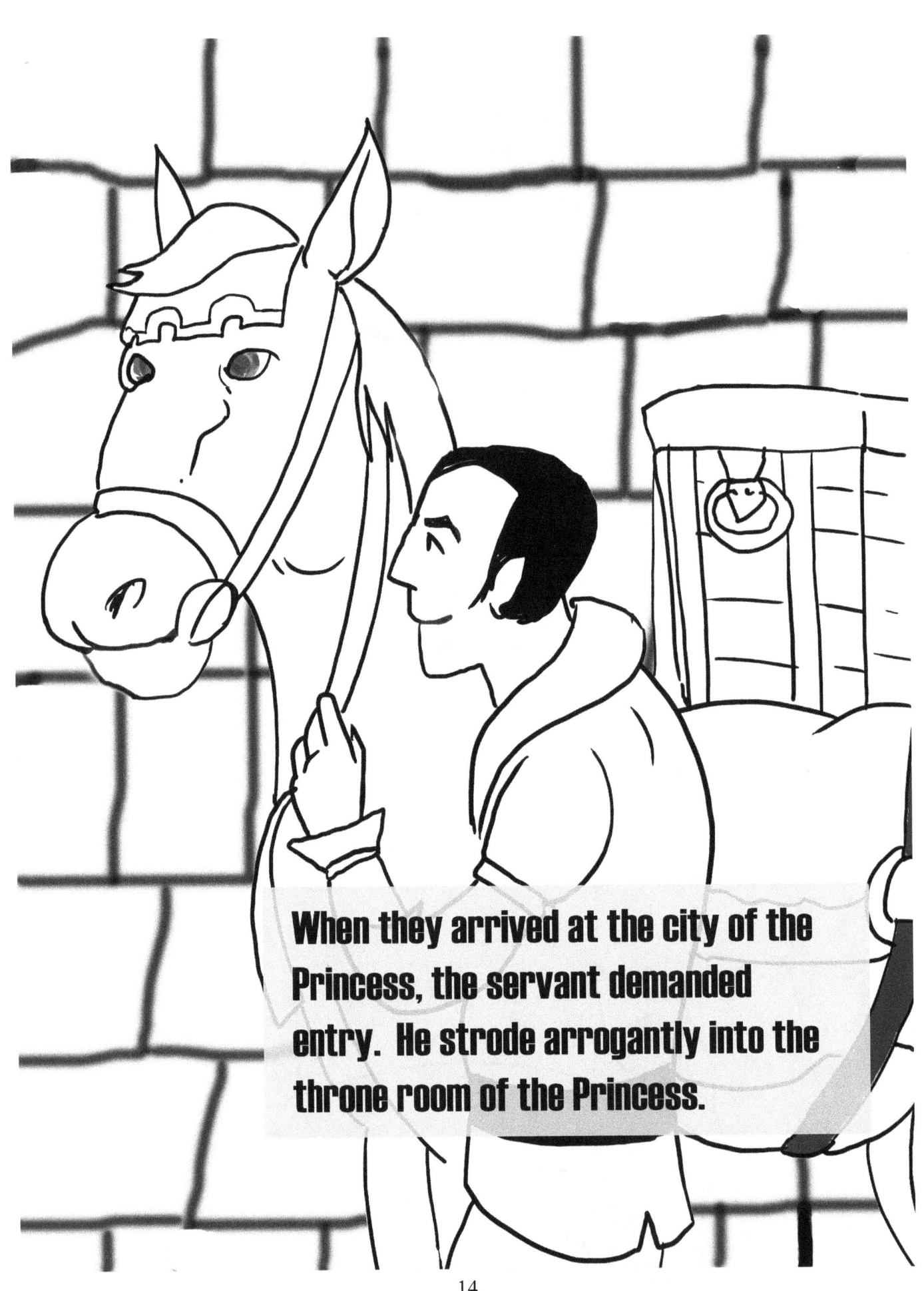

The servant proclaimed, "I have come from a far away land ruled by a great King. He sent me to ask you to be his wife. I come bearing a priceless gift for you."

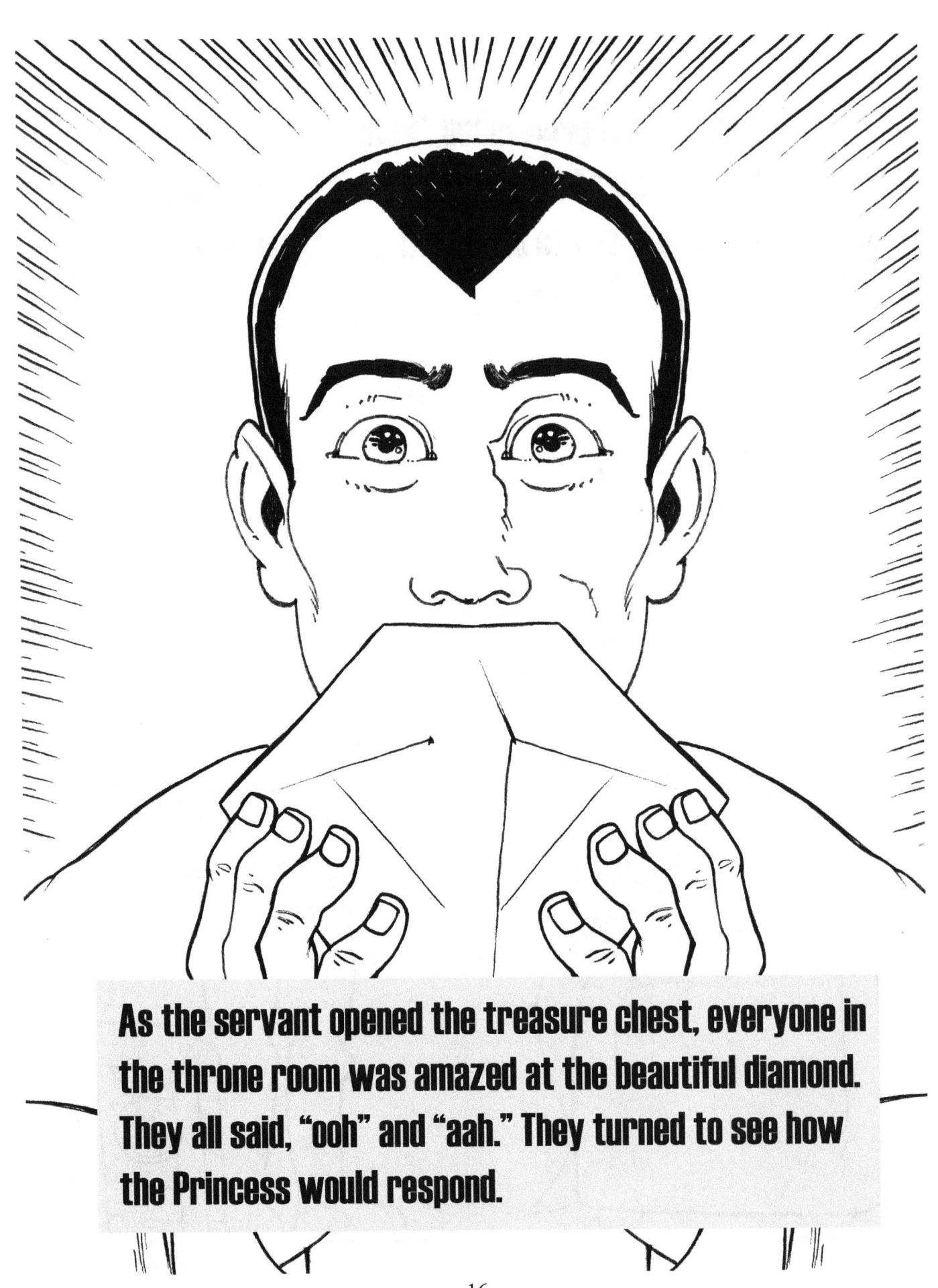

The servant traveled home very sad. He realized his mistake. His King had a wonderful heart that was full of love for people. The servant had become so proud of carrying the Gift of the King that he had forgotten to have the Heart of the King.

We serve a great King.
Our King has given each of us a gift.

Some have the gift of singing. Some have the gift of preaching. Some have the gift of performing miracles. Some are given the gift of intellect. Some have a gift for earning money. Others are given a gift of administration.

"But the gifts of the Spirit are given to each one for the profit of all: for to one is given the word of wisdom through the Spirit, to another the word of knowledge through the same Spirit, to another faith by the same Spirit, to another gifts of healings by the same Spirit, to another the working of miracles, to another prophecy, to another discerning of spirits, to another different kinds of tongues, to another the interpretation of tongues" (1 Corinthians 12:7-10)

But, no matter how great your gift is, it is far more important that you have the Heart of the King.

"But the fruit of the Spirit is love, joy, peace, patience, kindness, goodness, faithfulness, gentleness, self-control" (Galatians 5:22-23)

About the Author:

Daniel King:

* Has spoken to more than 2,000 live audiences in over 60 nations around the world.
* His Gospel Festivals regularly draw crowds in excess of 50,000 people.
* Preached his first public sermon at the age of six.
* Grew up working with his parents as a missionary in Mexico.
* Started his own ministry and begin traveling to churches across America at the age of sixteen.
* Daniel recently celebrated twenty years of full-time ministry.
* Graduated summa cum laude from Oral Roberts University in 2002 with a B.A. degree in New Testament Studies and a Master of Divinity degree in 2014.
* Set a goal at the age of fifteen to lead 1,000,000 people to Jesus before the age of thirty. With God's help, Daniel accomplished the goal of leading one million people in a prayer of salvation.
* Author of fourteen books including: The Secret of Obed-Edom, Healing Power, Fire Power, Soul Winning, and Grace Wins. Over 600,000 books in print.
* Has appeared on Daystar, TBN, TCT, Grace TV, and numerous other television and radio programs. He has been a guest lecturer at Oral Roberts University, Victory Bible College, Christ for the Nations Institute, Lionsgate Leadership School, and The Father's House Discipleship School.
* Has built three churches overseas.
* Founder and President of King Ministries International.
* Co-Founder of The Soul Winner's Alliance, an organization dedicated to training evangelists.
* Married Jessica on April 21, 2007. They have two children, Caleb and Katie Grace.

Our Goal?
Every Soul!

Daniel & Jessica King

Soul Winning Festivals

The vision of King Ministries is to lead 1,000,000 people to Jesus every year and to train believers to become leaders.

To contact Daniel & Jessica King:

Write:

King Ministries International

PO Box 701113

Tulsa, OK 74170 USA

King Ministries Canada

PO Box 3401

Morinville, Alberta T8R 1S3 Canada

Call toll-free:

1-877-431-4276

Visit us online:

www.kingministries.com

E-Mail:

daniel@kingministries.com

www.ingramcontent.com/pod-product-compliance
Lightning Source LLC
Chambersburg PA
CBHW081026040426
42444CB00014B/3370